sweetgrass and thyme

Joy McCall

sweetgrass and thyme

Cover art: 'Return' © Jonathan Day Art, Alpine Oregon, USA, 2017.

Etsy shop: *We Are Beautiful*

https://www.etsy.com/shop/jonathanday

for my nearest and dearest, with love

A Circling

perhaps a reed
still shrill with the wind,
yet silent
as the shrike's shadow
or an egret's stilted patience

Perhaps the doake made by a minnow sunning it-self in the shallows.

Or a hagstone, stray bone of field or foam, with a mouth to speak like the kill-hole in the Mimbres pot, made to set the spirit free from the red clay.

then what
of the sloughed skin
that says
incense was a snake here,
but left only dust?

I might say velvet because it calls to my finger-tips the mind of moss and the tine of the buck whose last prints vanished in a billow of snow.

or this cleat
of dirt from my boot
that holds the zwer
of a covey of partridge
loosed from the bracken.

What then? *What now?*

Joy McCall

The rusted hasp from a gate that never closed
again?

The little bell that knows the sheep trod of a thou-
sand moons?

or this shrew skull
that echoed with the mews
of a wheeling buzzard?
Life is, after all,
a circling

If I were to choose the shape of a thing,
it would be a poem by her hand.

~Claire Everett, North Yorkshire

sweetgrass and thyme

Joy McCall

so few the words
in the weight of days
one bright flower
among tall trees
peace, dropping slow*

*W. B. Yeats

lamplight in my eyes

sweetgrass and thyme

Han-shan watches
as I light the candle
and say
the resting prayer
for my kinfolk

Joy McCall

I wander
through the years
with wood and stone
in my hands
lamplight in my eyes

sweetgrass and thyme

summertime
insomnia
I beg the dark
come, fold yourself
around me

Joy McCall

the pond
is frozen
Orion
is glittering
high above the hut

sweetgrass and thyme

I wander
around the room
my fingers resting
on brass and copper
stone, wood and velvet

Joy McCall

over me hangs
the sword of Damocles
I balance
my father's heavy Bible
on my head

sweetgrass and thyme

a small book
in the man's pocket
the mouse sleeps
comforted by scraps
of quilt and poems

in the long grass

sweetgrass and thyme

spring water
trickling through the herb
in the copper sieve —
wild heartsease
the tea for dreamers

Joy McCall

when it rains
the scent of cloves
sweetgrass and earth
comes into my room
through the old floorboards

sweetgrass and thyme

I search
in the long grass
of the field
looking for words
that will abide

Joy McCall

long dry grasses
along the roadside
I want to lay down there
seeds falling soft
on my skin, in my hair

sweetgrass and thyme

tall grasses
moving slow
in the wind
a benediction
under the old oak

Joy McCall

sweetgrass
red cedar bark
juniper leaves
white sage, forest pine
and wild, wild thyme

sweetgrass and thyme

for so long
I carried burdens
in my cart
now it sits empty
home to spiders and moss

Joy McCall

in my head
a small squirrel
digging madly
for the right words —
the ones that rhyme

my own song

does the dove
watching the dusk owl,
long to hoot?
can I not be content
with my own song?

Joy McCall

two sides
of my mind
singing, dancing
a low sumac flute
a seven-stringed lyre

sweetgrass and thyme

when I'm gone
sing to me the songs
of the hilltop
of the old graves
the cedar boughs

Joy McCall

voices come
from the four corners
of the earth
on the wind, singing hymns
shanties and lullabies

sweetgrass and thyme

the holy night
the tribe gather
in the ruins
and sing the old songs
by the fire until dawn

Joy McCall

sometimes
the moors within him
are barren and bleak
no birds sing, the sheep
are on the far hills

sweetgrass and thyme

the grey witch
waves her bent hands
muttering —
ease and settle,
all troubles and woes

Joy McCall

I say the word
again and again
paralysed
it makes no sense
my spirit goes dancing

let us go now

sweetgrass and thyme

my heart
has many rooms
and over one doorway
is written *'let us go now*
*to Innisfree'**

*W. B. Yeats

Joy McCall

tidal surges
steal away the land
and uncover bones —
we trade man's grey roads
for mammoth skeletons

sweetgrass and thyme

I climb
thirsty and tired
and find again
the spring
rising from the rock

Joy McCall

I will go and hold out
my broken hands
and heart
to the gods of rain
and wind, on the hill

sweetgrass and thyme

the nomad
on the Siberian plain
gathers bones
I blow the wolverine whistle
the whole earth howls

Joy McCall

along the road
dark noisy crows
above the hay bales
a low bridge
a trickling creek

sweetgrass and thyme

roaming through
the wide landscape
musing on truth
in the sand at my feet
the word *trust*

Joy McCall

where the road
curves round the hill,
at the foot
of a split cedar
a deer, grazing

the shape of a thing

sweetgrass and thyme

there are times
when the shelter of trees
is enough
a shoulder to lean on
a hand to hold

Joy McCall

I wonder
about friendship
and find
the Olde English *sciepe* —
the shape of a thing

sweetgrass and thyme

my soul
wanting to go home
feels the pulling
of the river, the sea,
the field, the hedges

Joy McCall

reclaiming
the word *cripple*
for myself
I feel at home
in my flesh and bones

sweetgrass and thyme

below trees dripping rain
I sit, happy as a fish
in a flowing stream
calm as a pebble
on a quiet riverbed

Joy McCall

he lays his hand
gently on my shoulder
and I feel
the slow, quiet
unfurling of wings

sweetgrass and thyme

I ponder
enchantment
and sorcery
and the slow tears
run down my cheeks

Joy McCall

the poem, circling
winding through my days
has no end
and no beginning
no alpha, no omega

sweetgrass and thyme

I should like to lie on a bed
of freshly picked sweetgrass and thyme
the hedgewitch says as she hands me
a sprig of scented dreams

in my sleep I often see her
candlelit in her holy room
whispering rhymes into the smoke
from a small smudging bowl

~Liam Wilkinson, North Yorkshire

. . . something about Joy

Joy has wandered far and wide and come full circle back to where she was born, among the North Folk.

Along the way, she found loving souls, two wondrous daughters, good work, poetry and all kinds of living things.

She has written of these in many books.

Lately, after a near-fatal motorcycle crash, she goes about the byways in a chair with wheels.

Printed in Great Britain
by Amazon